D0624966

To Fred, who knows why, and to everyone
who fights to protect the diversity of life
on this planet.

Groundwood Books / House of Anansi Press
groundwoodbooks.com

We acknowledge for their financial support of our publishing program the Canada
Council for the Arts, the Ontario Arts Council and the Government of Canada.

Canada Council   Conseil des Arts
for the Arts   du Canada

ONTARIO ARTS COUNCIL
CONSEIL DES ARTS DE L'ONTARIO
an Ontario government agency
un organisme du gouvernement de l'Ontario

With the participation of the Government of Canada   Canadä
Avec la participation du gouvernement du Canada

Library and Archives Canada Cataloguing in Publication
Thornhill, Jan, author, illustrator
The tragic tale of the great auk / Jan Thornhill.
Issued in print and electronic formats.
ISBN 978-1-55498-865-5 (bound). — ISBN 978-1-55498-866-2 (pdf)
1. Great auk — Juvenile literature. 2. Great auk — Ecology —
Juvenile literature. 3. Extinct birds — Juvenile literature. I. Title.
QL696.C42T56 2016   j598.3'3   C2015-908450-4
C2015-908451-2

The illustrations for this book were created on computer by drawing and painting
with a stylus and tablet in Corel Painter, a natural media program.
Design by Michael Solomon
Printed and bound in Malaysia

MIX
Paper from
responsible sources
FSC
www.fsc.org   FSC® C012700

The Tragic Tale

OF THE

GREAT AUK

JAN THORNHILL

GROUNDWOOD BOOKS
HOUSE OF ANANSI PRESS
TORONTO   BERKELEY

BEHOLD THE GREAT AUK! The Gejrfugl! The northern penguin!

Less than four centuries ago, hundreds of thousands of these magnificent birds lived in the frigid seas between Europe and North America.

Now there are none.

So what happened?

It's a complicated story. Although humans — as you may suspect — did indeed have a heavy hand in the Great Auk's extinction, there were other factors that contributed to its demise, not the least of which was the bird's own anatomy and behavior.

In the cold North Atlantic, the Great Auk was the biggest bird around. It weighed as much as a sack of potatoes and stood as tall as a three-year-old. It had a formidable beak and strong webbed feet. A brilliant swimmer, it "flew" through the water as swiftly as the fish it hunted. It could hold its breath for minutes and could dive so deep it would disappear from sight. And it was long-lived — its lifespan was twenty years or more.

Sounds impressive, doesn't it?

But wait! There was a slight glitch in this expert fish-hunter's design. Over millions of years of evolution, its wings — though eventually perfect for propelling it underwater — became so stunted, so small, they couldn't get the bird off the ground.

The Great Auk couldn't fly to save its life. Literally.

Most of the time, being flightless wasn't a big deal.

As a true seabird, the Great Auk's home for ten months of the year was the open ocean, where it had no need to fly. When sleeping or at rest, in fine weather or foul, it floated on the surface, rising and falling with the swells. Its waterproof feathers and thick layer of fat kept it warm. When hungry, it dove, steering with its large webbed feet and flapping its tiny flattened wings to propel itself into the schools of fish it caught with its over-sized beak. It was so streamlined and so fast, it had no fear of predators at sea.

But when it was on land — *that* was another story.

As the Great Auk evolved into a lethal fisher, not only did its wings shrink, but its feet also gradually moved farther and farther back on its body. Having its feet so close to its tail made them perfect to use as a rudder. But they were not very useful for getting around on land. When the Great Auk struggled out of the water onto a rocky shore, it could only toddle along awkwardly in a fully upright position — so awkwardly that one of its earliest English names was The Wobble.

So why didn't The Wobble avoid land entirely?

The answer is simple. Birds can't lay their eggs in water. The Great Auk had no choice. Once a year, it had to clumsily hop out of the sea onto the rocky ledge of its birth, where it searched out its life partner. Once reunited, the couple rubbed their beaks together and nibbled each other's necks. Then they mated.

Not long afterwards, the female, wedged upright between innumerable other nesting auks, laid a single egg on bare rock. Both parents took turns brooding this precious egg — the only one they would produce all year — cradling it between their feet to keep it warm. Unlike most other birds' eggs, each Great Auk egg had markings that were distinctly different from any other — a handy way for each pair to recognize its own.

A month and a half later, the chick, covered in fluffy gray down, would crack through the shell. In less than two weeks it would be big enough to leave the rookery. Toddling alongside its parents to the water's edge, it would dive for the first time into its true home, the frigid waters of the North Atlantic.

At least five long years would pass before this fledgling would feel rock beneath its feet again, when it would finally be old enough to find a mate for itself.

For a mature Great Auk, spending almost two months ashore each year was a necessity. But it was a dangerous necessity. On land, it had little defense against the hungry jaws of wolves and foxes and polar bears. A puffin can hunker down in its burrow. A tern can dive-bomb an interloper and peck its skull with its pointed beak. A goose can cause serious damage to an attacker with its wings and bill, or it can simply fly away.

But all a flightless Great Auk could do when danger threatened was try to reach the safety of the sea, pathetically "running" towards the water about as fast as you can walk. There was little it could do to defend an egg or chick except angrily clack its beak.

How, then, did it so successfully raise its young for millennia?

It chose to nest in hard-to-get-to places — shorelines protected by looming cliffs or small rocky islands surrounded by swirling currents — isolated places that carnivorous land mammals couldn't easily reach. So for many thousands of years it thrived.

But then, out of the blue, a new class of predator arrived — a class of clever hunters that, like the Great Auk, walked upright. Our early human ancestors.

During the last Ice Age, when much of northern Europe and most of Canada lay frozen beneath a half mile of ice, the oceans were colder, so the Great Auk was found farther south. Five thousand years before the glaciers retreated, a group of Stone Age humans entered a cave not far from the Mediterranean. They mixed charcoal and red-ochre pigment into paint, then used crude brushes and their fingertips to make images of the animals they hunted.

They painted ibex and bison. They painted wild horses and big-antlered deer.

And they painted Great Auks.

Paleontologists have found other signs that early humans enjoyed eating fire-roasted Great Auk just as much as we enjoy eating barbecued chicken today. Numerous tool-marked remains of the bird's big bones have been unearthed from ancient fire pits and trash heaps on both sides of the Atlantic, up and down the coasts. Some charred bones are almost ninety thousand years old.

Until these early hunters and gatherers learned to construct rafts and crude boats, they were only able to catch the Great Auk on its mainland nesting grounds. Traveling in small family groups, with unsophisticated methods of preserving meat and eggs, they were barely able to make a dent in the total number of Great Auks. But they definitely ate them.

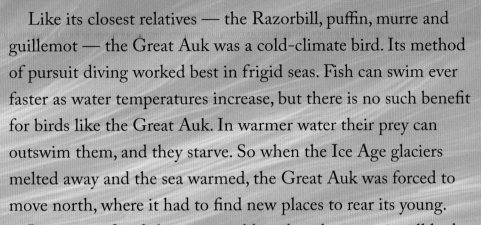

Like its closest relatives — the Razorbill, puffin, murre and guillemot — the Great Auk was a cold-climate bird. Its method of pursuit diving worked best in frigid seas. Fish can swim ever faster as water temperatures increase, but there is no such benefit for birds like the Great Auk. In warmer water their prey can outswim them, and they starve. So when the Ice Age glaciers melted away and the sea warmed, the Great Auk was forced to move north, where it had to find new places to rear its young.

Its cousins faced the same problem, but these species all had the luxury of flight, which allowed them to nest in places that land predators, including humans, couldn't easily reach — ledges on the faces of towering cliffs, for instance. Not the Great Auk, though, which not only couldn't fly, but was also a poor climber.

It had to be able to ride the surf or waddle out of the ocean — no matter how high or low the tide — onto a place flat enough to lay an egg. And because it couldn't fly miles away to find food for itself and, eventually, its ravenous chick, it could only nest where there was a reliable supply of fish in the waters surrounding the rookery.

These were persnickety needs. In the North Atlantic, not a lot of places fit the bill, especially when even small climate changes could alter ocean currents and, in turn, the locations of the auk's prey. Even so, the Great Auk thrived.

But then humans became seafarers.

On the east side of the North Atlantic, a culture arose that eventually conquered the northern seas. Long before these people were called Vikings, they regularly ate the Great Auk, which they called the Gejrfugl, or spear-bird. But as the climate gradually warmed, the Great Auk slowly disappeared, and by the time the Vikings pushed west in sail-propelled *knarrs*, the Great Auk had long since vanished from Scandinavia.

Once the Vikings settled in Iceland, though, they discovered rookeries on coastal headlands and nearby skerries — uninhabitable rocks that jutted above the waves. As always, the flightless bird was easy to catch, but only when a nesting colony was easy to get to. Luckily for the Great Auk, several of its Icelandic rookeries were surrounded by such treacherous currents and crashing surf, even the bravest Norseman didn't dare go near them. So in Iceland, the Great Auk survived.

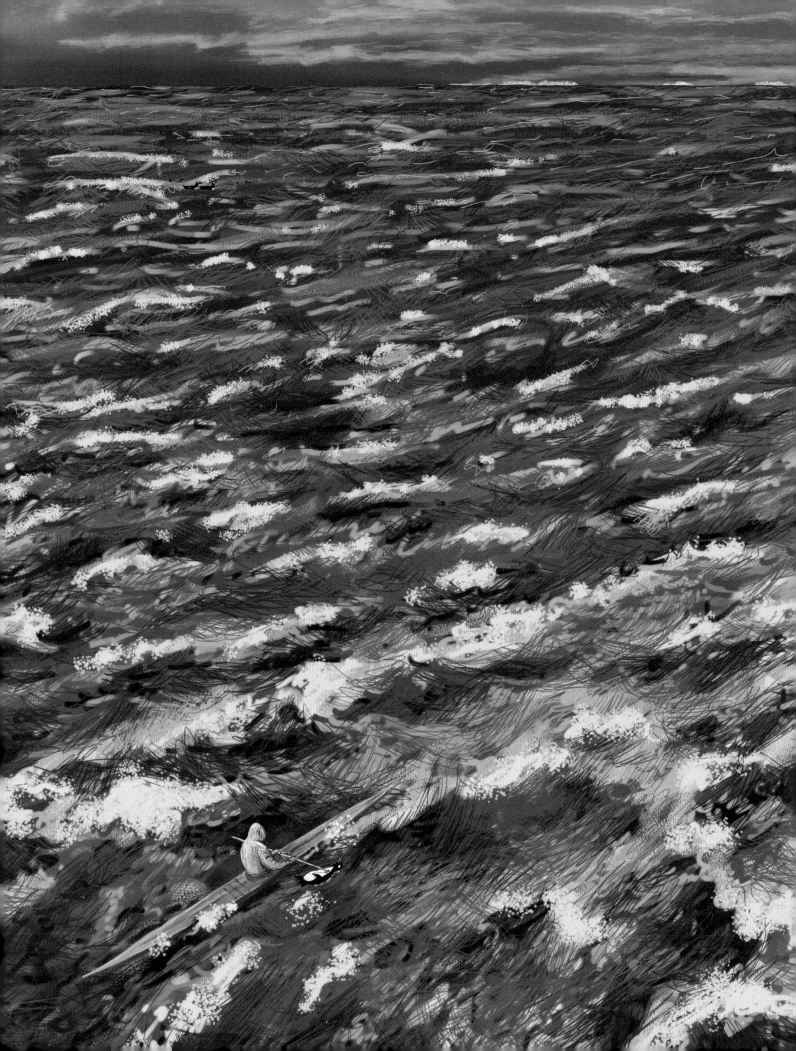

Meanwhile, on the west coast of Greenland, Inuit also ate the bird they called Isarukitsoq, or stump-winged. But because the area had such a healthy population of polar bears, the auk avoided nesting there, so Inuit could only hunt it at sea. Cutting through the waves in their kayaks, hunters looking for seals would come across small flotillas of auks in the open ocean and would spear them with bird darts — specialized harpoons.

These people tell the legend of a group of kayak hunters who were overcome by a sudden storm far from land. Many drowned. One of the survivors, before he reached home, speared a Great Auk. Somehow, he lost his paddle. He used the bird's buoyant body to keep his kayak from capsizing until he reached shore.

As well as eating all edible parts of the Great Auk, Greenland Inuit fashioned warm underwear from its skins (worn with the feathers facing inwards) and used the black skin of its webbed feet to decorate sealskin bags. They even had a use for the bird's windpipe, which they inflated and attached to a bladder dart — another kind of harpoon.

Farther south in Newfoundland lived the Beothuk, descendants of earlier Aboriginal people who so revered the Great Auk that they buried a man in an outfit decorated with more than two hundred auk beaks. The Beothuk, who painted every inch of their skin, as well as their belongings, with red-ochre pigment each spring, invented a unique crescent-shaped canoe specifically to reach island colonies of the bird they called Apponath.

With no maps or instruments to guide them, Beothuk men daringly paddled for two days straight out into the open ocean to reach one particular island that supported a massive colony of thousands of Great Auks. The only way they could keep their canoes upright in the rough seas was to fill the bottoms with rocks. For the return journey, the rocks were replaced with the same weight in dead Great Auks and their eggs.

The Beothuk ate the meat fresh, and they dried the yolks of the eggs to add to soups and sausages, which provided them with fat and protein throughout the winter.

But only a few canoes might make the dangerous journey to the island each year. So in its western range, there were still hundreds of thousands of Great Auks.

But then the Europeans arrived.

Five hundred years ago, it took almost two months for a ship to sail from Europe to North America. By the end of such a long voyage with no refrigeration, a ship's crew was sick to death of eating only hardtack — a tooth-cracking biscuit — and salted pork or mutton.

Imagine their delight when they came across islands so jam-packed with nesting birds the men could barely find spots to place their feet. Big meaty birds. Meaty birds that couldn't fly. It was like a gift from God.

Some of these men called the bird Garefowl. Others called it Pingwen, or white-front, a name that became "penguin" years before other sailors encountered a similar but completely unrelated bird in the southern seas.

For three centuries, the crew of every ship that arrived slaughtered the original penguin by the boatload, clubbing or strangling it to death. They ate it fresh and they ate it after salting it in barrels. They plucked it and used its feathers to stuff quilts, pillows and mattresses. They boiled it in huge iron cauldrons to loosen its feathers and release its fat to use as lamp oil. When driftwood ran out on the treeless islands, the cauldron fires were fueled with the Great Auk itself. It was so fatty it was flammable.

And they collected its eggs — by the thousands — each half as big again as a goose's. These were sold in the fast-growing towns that had sprung up all along the eastern seaboard of North America. For two centuries, June was the month for auk-egg omelets and yellow pancakes made rich with yolks so thick they had to be watered down before being mixed into the batter.

For more than two hundred years the Great Auk and its eggs were so plentiful it seemed the supply would never run out. Then its numbers began to dwindle. Noticeably. By the end of the 1600s, all but one of its western nesting colonies had completely collapsed. It was simple arithmetic. Every egg eaten was an egg that would never hatch, and every Great Auk killed was a Great Auk that would never again rear young.

The last stronghold was the island off the coast of Newfoundland that the Beothuk had canoed to every year,

where uncountable numbers of Great Auks had once nested. Known as Funk Island for its funky bird-dropping smell, by the late 1700s it was home to only a few hundred pairs of auks each spring.

There was an attempt to save the Funk Island auk. A petition was issued that banned both killing it for its feathers and stealing its eggs. The penalty was public flogging. It was one of the earliest efforts to save an endangered animal.

But it came too late. By 1800, not a single pair could be found nesting on the island.

But the Great Auk was not yet extinct. Off the coast of
Iceland, there was one last colony that nested every year on a
tiny skerry that jutted out of the sea — Geirfuglasker, named for
the bird.

Iceland lies on one of Earth's volcanic hotspots. Geirfuglasker
was part of a string of lava-rock skerries that had been pushed
above the waves by volcanic activity. Surrounded by fierce
currents, treacherous surf and unpredictable winds, it was almost
impossible to get to. Unless you were a seabird that could fly. Or
a brilliant swimmer like the Great Auk.

This last nesting colony could only be raided when the seas
were calm, which was a rare occurrence. So for many years the
Great Auk had a safe haven. But then disaster struck. In 1830,
a violent volcanic eruption caused the unimaginable to happen.
Geirfuglasker disappeared beneath the waves. Completely.

The Great Auk had to find a new place to nest each spring.
It chose nearby Eldey Island. But there was a problem with this
choice. Eldey was much easier for people to get to.

Since the decimation of the Funk Island colony, the Great Auk had lost its value as a source of food or feathers or oil. But now it had a new value, and a much greater one: it had become so rare it was a collectible. Museums and private collectors were willing to pay steep prices for Great Auk skins, which were stuffed and mounted for display, often alongside one of the bird's eggs.

When weather permitted, expeditions set out for Eldey with the sole purpose of capturing and killing the few surviving birds to sell to collectors. In 1831, twenty-four were taken. By 1840, the number of auks on the island was down to three.

That same year, a stray Great Auk was captured on a rock near St Kilda, Scotland, where generations before there had once been a nesting colony. Three days later, a terrible storm came out of nowhere. The islanders, convinced that their captive had conjured up the tempest, declared it a witch and stoned it to death. This was the last Great Auk ever seen alive in the British Isles.

But it was not the last Great Auk.

One June day in 1844, three Icelandic men, hired by a Great Auk dealer in Denmark, scrambled from a small boat onto Eldey Island. They were in luck. In the middle of a crowd of brooding Razorbills and murres stood two much larger birds. The last known pair of Great Auks.

One was quickly cornered and captured. The second
toddled away from its pursuers as fast as it could, but it was
trapped against a cliff face it could not climb, and it, too, was
caught. Both birds were strangled. On their way back to the
boat with their prizes, the men spotted a single auk egg lying
on the lava-rock ledge. A broken egg.

For years, people scoured the North Atlantic for other Great Auks to kill and sell, but they found none.

Egg collecting at the time was a popular hobby. Before bird protection laws came into play, thousands of oologists around the world climbed trees, scaled cliffs and squished through swamps to rob birds' nests of their eggs. The rich and the lazy simply paid others for the eggs their collections were missing. The rarer a bird, the more coveted its egg. The more coveted an egg, the higher its value. And what could be more valuable to an egg collector than the egg of an extinct bird?

By the end of the 1800s, the same money paid for a single Great Auk egg could have paid for two or three modest houses. The eggs were so rare that one wealthy collector bought an egg and immediately smashed it, simply to drive up the price of another he already owned. Another fanatical collector eventually managed to acquire a total of thirteen eggs. The man, who was a bit of an eccentric, never displayed his eggs, but kept them — with half a million other bird eggs — hidden away in boxes until he died.

Along with the seventy-three Great Auk eggs that are known to exist today, there are also seventy-eight stuffed birds. Almost all the birds were killed in Iceland, many on Eldey Island.

Some of these mounted auks have extravagant stories of multiple owners, of traveling back and forth across the Atlantic, of being spirited to secret hiding places to protect them from bombs during wars. One was once owned by John James Audubon. He famously painted life-size portraits of four hundred species of North American birds in the early 1800s, but never saw a living Great Auk. Yet another is a bird that had been found starving off the coast of Ireland in 1834, and was kept as a pet for a few months before it died. It was

fed fresh fish and potatoes mashed with milk, and is said to have followed its keeper around like a dog.

But perhaps the most celebrated stuffed Great Auk is the one that the Icelandic government bought in 1971. They paid so much for it that it was featured on the cover of the *Guinness Book of World Records*. Until that time, Iceland, the last place the Great Auk had lived, owned no examples of the iconic bird. It was such an important acquisition for the country that children were given a half-day holiday from school and a red carpet was laid out at the airport to greet its arrival. A bird that never flew in life flew into Iceland strapped into its very own seat on an airplane.

So is that all that's left of the Great Auk? A few sad taxidermy displays and blown eggs?

Surprisingly, no. The Great Auk is gone but, in interesting ways, it lives on. The ecosystem it was once part of still exists. The fish it ate, the other seabirds it shared its nesting grounds with still live in the North Atlantic, and some have benefited directly from the Great Auk's extinction.

Funk Island, once home to the largest Great Auk nesting colony, now supports more than a million nesting seabirds every spring. One species is a relatively new arrival — the Atlantic Puffin.

Puffins dig burrows for their eggs. During the years that Funk Island was home to the Great Auk, there was not a single nesting puffin, because there was no soil for puffins to excavate. But now there is.

So where did this new soil come from?

During the time of the Great Auk slaughter, when uncountable numbers of auks were boiled for oil and plucked of their feathers, their carcasses were simply tossed aside on the bare rock. By the thousands. Over time, these grisly remains gradually decomposed into a thick layer of humus, soil that's excavated into burrows by more than two thousand pairs of puffins every year. A gift from the grave.

But an even greater gift from the Great Auk is that Funk Island is now a protected ecological reserve. No one is allowed on the island other than scientific researchers. The birds of Funk can raise their young in peace.

When the Great Auk disappeared, there was little public outcry, and the world didn't stop. Instead, Razorbills, guillemots and other seabirds immediately replaced the Great Auk as new targets for feather and egg harvesting. In a few short years an astonishing number of these birds were killed.

By the 1860s, it seemed obvious to a handful of people that, if nothing was done, many more species would soon meet the fate of the Great Auk. A group of scientists and other concerned citizens lobbied the British government and, finally, in 1869, an act banning the killing of thirty-three species during their nesting seasons was introduced.

The conservation movement was born. All over the world, more laws protecting other wildlife would follow, often spurred by grassroots movements of ordinary people — people who believe it should be possible to share this planet with a multitude of other species. Ordinary and remarkable people like you.

Greenland

Iceland

Eldey Island

Geirfuglasker

St Kilda

British Isles

North America

Funk Island

Newfoundland

North Atlantic Ocean

Europe

Cosquer Cave (prehistoric paintings)

Scandinavia

Mediterranean Sea

GLOSSARY

Beothuk – Aboriginal people who lived in what is now Newfoundland, Canada, the last of whom died in 1829

fledgling – a young bird whose baby down is being replaced with adult feathers

Ice Age – popular name for the most recent glacial period that ended 12,000 years ago

Inuit – Indigenous peoples inhabiting the Arctic from Greenland across northern Canada to Alaska

knarr – a Viking cargo ship used for long voyages

Norsemen – the group of people who spoke Old Norse between the 8th and 11th centuries (700–1100)

oologist – someone who collects eggs and nests or studies the eggs and nests of birds

paleontologist – someone who studies the fossilized remains of living things

rookery – a place where large numbers of seabirds nest

skerry – a tiny, uninhabitable rock island

Stone Age – prehistoric era when early humans made tools and weapons from stone

taxidermy – the art of stuffing and mounting animal skins for display

Vikings – Scandinavian raiders and traders whose culture thrived from the 8th to 11th centuries (700-1100)

Puffin   Tern   Gannet   Razorbill   Murre   Guillemot   Great Auk

NAMES FOR THE GREAT AUK

Pinguinus impennis (Latin, scientific name)
Isarukitsoq (Greenland Inuit)
Apponath (Beothuk)
Gejrfugl (Old Norse, Danish)
Geirfugl (Icelandic)
Great Auk, Garefowl (English)
Pingwen (Welsh)

Grand pingouin (French)
The Wobble (New England)
Falcóg mhór (Irish)
Reuzenalk (Dutch)
Riesenalk, Meegans (German)
Alca gigante, Gran pingüino (Spanish)

LIST OF EXTINCT SPECIES

Despite our growing understanding of the importance of ecology and conservation, animals have continued to disappear around the world since the demise of the Great Auk. This is only a partial list of species that have been driven to extinction by human actions since 1844. If you look them up, you will find that each of these animals, like the Great Auk, has its own tragic tale to tell.

B=Bird   M=Mammal   O=Other (Reptile, Amphibian, Fish, Crustacean, Insect)

1850s Carpathian Wisent (Europe) M	1950s Caribbean Monk Seal (Caribbean) M
1860s Sea Mink (North America) M	Goff's Pocket Gopher (Florida, USA) M
1870s North Island Snipe (New Zealand) B	1960s Barbary Lion (North Africa) M
New Zealand Quail (New Zealand) B	*Hemigrapsus estellinensis* — Cave Crab
Falkland Islands Wolf (Falkland Islands) M	(Texas, USA) O
Eastern Elk (North America) M	Huia (New Zealand) B
Ula-ai-hawane (Hawaii, USA) B	South Island Snipe (New Zealand) B
Atlas Bear (North Africa) M	1970s Caspian Tiger (Mideast/Asia) M
1880s Quagga (South Africa) M	Guam Flying Fox (Guam) M
1890s Chatham Fernbird (New Zealand) B	Japanese Sea Lion (Sea of Japan) M
Gull Island Vole (New York, USA) M	Yunnan Lake Newt (China) O
1900s Stephens Island Wren (New Zealand) B	1980s Formosan Clouded Leopard (Taiwan) M
Piopio (New Zealand) B	Gastric-brooding frogs (Australia) O
Rocky Mountain Locust (Western USA & Canada) O	Dusky Seaside Sparrow (Florida, USA) B
Bulldog Rat (Christmas Island) M	Amistad Gambusia Fish (Texas, USA) O
Chatham Bellbird (New Zealand) B	2000s Cebu Warty Pig (Philippines) M
Tarpan Horse (Russia) M	Baiji River Dolphin (China) M
1910s Passenger Pigeon (North America) B	Saudi Gazelle (Arabian Peninsula) M
Laughing Owl (New Zealand) B	2010s Western Black Rhinoceros (Indonesia) M
1920s Pasadena Freshwater Shrimp (California, USA) O	Javan Tiger (Indonesia) M
Syrian Wild Ass (Jordan) M	Eastern Sumatran Rhinoceros — extinct in the wild,
Caucasian Wisent (Eastern Europe) M	but three in captivity (Indonesia) M
1930s Tasmanian Tiger or Wolf (Tasmania) M	Pinta Island Tortoise (Galapagos Islands, Ecuador) O
O'o (Hawaii, USA) B	
Bali Tiger (Bali, Indonesia) M	
Dwarf Hutia (Cuba) M	
Schomburgk's Deer (Thailand) M	
Carolina Parakeet (Eastern USA) B	
1940s Wake Island Rail (Wake Island) B	
Bushwren (New Zealand) B	

RESOURCES

The Great Auk: messybeast.com/extinct/great-auk.htm
Seabirds: hww.ca/en/wildlife/birds/seabirds.html
Aquatic species of North Atlantic (no birds, though!): dfo-mpo.gc.ca/species-especes/aquatic-aquatique/browse-consultez-eng.htm
Threatened species: worldwildlife.org/species/directory?direction=desc&sort=extinction_status
The Beothuk: heritage.nf.ca/browser/theme/520
And just for fun — and thought!:
Aviary Wonders Inc.: Spring Catalog and Instruction Manual by Kate Samworth, Clarion Books, 2014.

For older readers

The Great Auk: The Extinction of the Original Penguin by Errol Fuller, Bunker Hill Publishing, 2003.

The Sixth Extinction: An Unnatural History by Elizabeth Kolbert, Henry Holt and Co., 2014.

"When the Last of the Great Auks Died, It Was by the Crush of a Fisherman's Boot" by Samantha Galasso, Smithsonian.com, smithsonianmag.com/smithsonian-institution/with-crush-fisherman-boot-the-last-great-auks-died-180951982/?no-ist, July 10, 2014.

ACKNOWLEDGMENTS

My thanks to Bill Montevecchi (Memorial University, St. John's, Newfoundland) and to the fabulous team at Groundwood Books!

REFERENCES

Articles

Bengtson, Sven-Axel. "Breeding Ecology and Extinction of the Great Auk (*Pinguinus impennis*): Anecdotal Evidence and Conjectures." *The Auk*, Vol. 101, January 1984, pp. 1-12.

Birkhead, Tim. "How Collectors Killed the Great Auk." *New Scientist*, Vol. 142, No. 1927, May 28, 1994, pp. 24-27.

d'Errico, Francesco. "Birds of the Grotte Cosquer: the Great Auk and Palaeolithic Prehistory." *Antiquity*, Vol. 68, No. 258, March 1994, pp. 39-47.

Galasso, Samantha. "When the Last of the Great Auks Died, It Was by the Crush of a Fisherman's Boot." Smithsonian.com, smithsonianmag.com/smithsonian-institution/with-crush-fisherman-boot-the-last-great-auks-died-180951982/?no-ist, July 10, 2014.

Kirkham, I.R., and W.A. Montevecchi. "The Breeding Birds of Funk Island, Newfoundland: An Historical Perspective." *American Birds*, Vol. 36, March 1982, pp. 111-118.

Meldgaard, Morten. "The Great Auk, *Pinguinus impennis*, in Greenland." *Historical Biology*, Vol. 1, No. 2, 1988, pp. 145-178.

Montevecchi, W.A., and D.A. Kirk. "Great Auk (*Pinguinus impennis*)." The Birds of North America Online (A. Poole, Ed.), Cornell Lab of Ornithology, http://bna.birds.cornell.edu/bna/species/260/articles/introduction, 1996.

Books

Fuller, Errol. *The Great Auk* (illustrated ed.). New York: Harry N. Abrams, 1999.

Grieve, Symington. *The Great Auk, or Garefowl: Its history, archaeology, and Remains.* 1885. Cambridge University Press, 2015.

Montevecchi, W.A., and L.M. Tuck. *Newfoundland Birds: Exploitation, Study, Conservation.* Cambridge: Nuttall Ornithological Club, Harvard University, 1987.

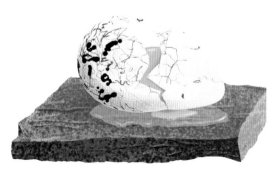